Medulloblastoma and I

A Journey through Brain Cancer

Gari Wellingham

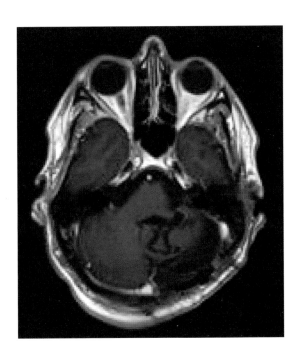

Dedications

Not to be melodramatic, but I owe a HUGE debt to anyone who even remotely has touched my Cancer experience.

The NHS are a sensational organisation, and any apparent criticism in this account is made out of love. They've not only saved my life (for 'free'), but I've had the pleasure of meeting so many people working for this great institution who have inspired me and made life easier for me, that I think that we, as a nation, should give a lot more recognition to this service. It's not perfect, but hey, are any of us?

Of course, my friends and family have been through the wringer with this too. I thank them massively for their love, kind words and for allowing me the space to approach them with updates "as-and-when" rather than demanding updates constantly.

The real hero in this story is my wonderful (now husband) Max.

I cannot even begin to explain his stunning contribution to my being here to write this all down. If you can think of it, he did it. I can never repay the debt that I owe him, and the fact that he doesn't see it in this way, only makes me love him even more.

Finally, this story is also for you – thank you for taking an interest in my ramblings. It's incredibly humbling to know that you're out there.

Introduction

A massive thank you to you for picking up my story.

The honest truth is that I never really intended to write this. I was responding to a written question" Tell me about your Cancer experience" and my response got a little out of hand, and thus my story was 'born'.

Throughout my Cancer experience, I have been genuinely bowled over by the care, love and concern from not just my nearest and dearest, but people all over the world.

My website http://garidavies.me.uk has effectively been my venting outlet during these times and you can find more of my experiences there too, including updates on 'what happened next'.

Unsurprisingly, my outlook on life has completely changed following this experience, and dare I say it, possibly for the better. Please don't take offense at this viewpoint (or any other in my story), Cancer is still a terrible, cruel and vicious disease, and I'd never wish it on anyone.

I can't promise that this account will be either engaging or well-written, but it's genuinely my story and typed using just my right hand and in my own words.

I will be donating the proceeds of this book to **The Brain Tumour Charity** who have been of great support.

The main thing that I'd like to get across is simply:
"Don't worry about a receiving a Cancer diagnosis, you could also get hit by a bus tomorrow!".

About The Brain Tumour Charity

- We are committed to having the biggest possible impact for everyone affected by a brain tumour, to defending the most amazing part of the human body, so that the diagnosis of a brain tumour is no longer a death sentence.

- We fight brain tumours on all fronts through research, awareness and support to save lives and improve quality of life.

- We fund pioneering research to find new treatments, improve understanding, increase survival rates and bring us closer to a cure.

- We raise awareness of the symptoms and effects of brain tumours, to reduce diagnosis times and make a difference every day to the lives of people with a brain tumour and their families.

- We provide support and information for anyone affected to improve quality of life.

https://www.thebraintumourcharity.org/about-us/who-we-are/

Chapter 1

OK, so my journey with cancer has been an 'experience' that I can tell you:

It all began whilst I was holidaying on a trip of a lifetime to Australia. I'd literally raided my savings accounts and gone alone as my now husband, Max, doesn't like flying. So there I was, 15,000 miles away from home and on the last day of my vacation, I suddenly got searing head pain. Now, never having had a migraine before, I just wrote it off to the heat of the Australian summer and went for a lie down. Later that night, I was out dancing in a disco to Kylie songs with not a care in the world.

Back home in England just a week later, and I had to come home from work. Once again, I was in absolute agony "deep inside my head". I went to the GP, who ran all the usual tests, and declared migraine. I was prescribed some beta blockers to see if they would help, and was duly sent on my merry way. Over the next 48 hours I continued to experience the pain and the beta blockers were sending me balmy, so I went back to the GP another two times, saw two different GPs and once again received a diagnosis of migraines.

The next morning was a Wednesday, I awoke late and I knew straight away something had changed. My pain was unbearable and I was being sick and had little to no balance (not a great combination by the way!). I rang NHS111 and was told to see someone ASAP. Unfortunately, by the time I rang, my GP had left and so I was directed to a Boots Walk-In service.

Once there, I waited three hours to see someone who was immediately concerned but not enough to stop her from apologising for what she was about to do – send me to hospital. On reflection, this "inconvenience" as she so strangely put it, saved my life!

Instead of going by ambulance, I had to make my own way on the Number 67 bus to Salford Royal, in pain, feeling sick and with zero balance. Rather stupidly, I also sat upstairs. I must have been a terrifying sight for those who saw me – hopefully nobody assumed I was just some crazy drunk!

Once at Salford Royal, I presented at A&E, was duly given a paracetamol by the triage nurse and left in the waiting room for 4 hours. After he'd finished work, and guided by the non-urgency of the earlier diagnosis, at about 6pm, Max came to wait with me. At this point, neither of us was particularly concerned.

An A&E doctor finally turned up and ran a whole load of assessments on me, including a CT scan, and just before midnight (shortly after Max had to leave), I was taken into a small windowless room and told that they were very concerned about fluid build-up in parts of my brain. Rather strangely, all I could say to the doctor as she told me this was "thank you" – it was something, and now I finally knew what. I felt strangely vindicated if only for that moment. She obviously knew that that she was delivering potentially bad news and I think my enlightened 'thanks' confused the heck out of her. I needed to have an MRI, but that could only happen in the morning, so I had to be admitted for the night.

Throughout the night, I was kept company by a lovely nurse who realised I'd had nothing to eat all day, so gave me a good feed before I was placed 'nil by mouth'. The bed room was a two-person room with just me in it, and an en-suite bathroom between the two beds. After advice from the nurse, I found myself hanging out of the bathroom window as this proved to be the only place where I could get a signal, and I called Max to update him.

Little did I know that this was going to be the last time that I'd speak with him before I came close to losing my life.

Incredibly happy In Australia just 24 hours before the
migraines were to start.

Chapter 2

The following morning, I was awoken by a team of hospital porters as soon as the MRI suite opened, and rushed through for a scan. When I say rushed through, we really were going at some fair rate, I nearly fell out of the wheelchair on several occasions!

After the scan, I returned to my room, and went straight to the bathroom to take a shower, after being advised that I should pounce on any chance to shower that I could find. I'm glad that I did, as it was to be the last shower that I'd have in three weeks. It wasn't luxurious, but it was a million times better than awkward basin washes in NHS grade bathrooms.

When I came out of the shower, there were three very sober looking people waiting for me at the foot of my bed, which took me rather by surprise… in fact, it was terrifying.

One chap introduced himself as a senior neurosurgeon, the other chap as his registrar along with a young lady who would also be working on my situation. Within 30 seconds of meeting these people, and whilst still wrapped in a towel, I was hearing fancy medical words of more than four syllables, a long spiel about what was going to happen, asked to sign lots of forms, and I was told that I needed to call my family immediately. I later learnt that they were so forceful about me doing this as they thought that I probably wouldn't make the operation. It was an odd experience calling my family as everyone was already at work and not accepting calls. Thankfully, I managed to get through to my little sister, Hannah (who was on a beach miles away in Blackpool, of all places), and pass a message on, including, bizarrely, the senior neurosurgeon's mobile phone number.

I wasn't able to speak to Max, I was told that there was no time and that the male registrar would ring him to explain what was going on. To this day, I regret not forcing the point that I wanted to speak with Max himself.

Chapter 3

I was literally picked up by porters wheeling my bed down the corridor at the nurses' station. I wasn't even allowed to walk the ten feet back to my room. They were in such a hurry to get me in to theatre that those last moments of 'normality' never really existed.

The entrance to the theatre prep area was slightly intimidating as you could see a large number of people at the other end of the room wielding knives and other such fear inducing equipment and not being particularly subtle about it. Speed affords no sensitivity.

I was wheeled in to the anaesthetists' area and put to sleep, whilst we were joking about the scary looking blokes outside. I was terrified, I'll admit, but everything was happening so quickly that I didn't have time to feel anything other than 'now'.

At this point, I feel I must share that I'd never even been in hospital before. I'd never broken anything, I'd never been seriously ill, and I'd never been rushed in to hospital in an ambulance on a drunken night out.

The next eleven hours (it was planned to be seven) I thankfully cannot remember anything of thanks to the sleepy juice. My Mum later told me that the senior neurosurgeon himself kept coming out to speak with my family, and told them that I was unlikely to make it through, and prepared everyone for the worst. My Mum would later comment how surreal it was to see his fancy leather shoes covered in my blood, so I guess I owe Mr Patel a new pair, if not my life!

Chapter 4

I cannot describe the agony that I felt when I was coming round after the operation. I had no real control of any of my limbs, and the bed felt like molten rubber - I honestly felt that aliens had experimented on me and made me in to some sort of weird being. I was screaming blue murder and I had to be knocked out again as I'm told the sounds that normally quiet old me made were terrifying.

When I came around it was spectacular. I was so thirsty after so long in surgery. I asked for water and promptly was allowed to down 3L. Now, anaesthetic will make you vomit as it leaves your system. Typically, I needed to chunder just as the nurse left my station and I hadn't got a sick bowl. 3L of water came back up and went all over the ICU. Not one of my finest moments but all I had to say was "I tried to warn you!!"

The next morning, I woke up, thinking that it was two days after - I didn't connect until the end of the day that my surgery had been the day before and my vomiting only hours before. Everything felt completely different.

The ICU unit was a bit of a scary place – there were a lot of people in there who were in a terrible state. I remember turning to my Mum and saying 'Thank God I'm not surrounded by all those computers and hooked up to all those space age looking horror machines!", to which Mum replied "Gari, you are!". Even in my current state, I still don't think that I had grasped the enormity of what had just happened in the last twelve hours.

At this point, I was allowed as much liquid morphine as I wanted, but the problem is that it was so hard to resist – they make it so damn tasty! At lunchtime, I was offered food to see if I could manage anything by a kindly nurse and my old love of jelly was reignited. This lovely nurse left me with three pots of the stuff and a knowing wink. She'd visit with more jelly throughout the day, and I'd really look forward to her coming more than the doctor with all the fancy drugs.

At tea time, my mother nearly killed me.

Chapter 5

Despite, miraculously, being able to co-ordinate the use of a knife and fork only 24 hours after brain surgery, I decided to try some mashed potato for my dinner. Mum was by the bedside, and was doing what all mothers do, fuss. She insisted on trying to spoon-feed me, despite my protestations. In the end it was easier to just give in to try and quell the worry and maternal instinct. For reasons that to this day none of us can fathom, Mum decided to load up an extra large spoon of mash, which went in too fast and caused me to choke and splutter – the whole time, I was worrying about my brains shooting out of the back of my head from the site of the operation. I'd like to say that this was a one off, but last year, she did exactly the same thing to my sister. It's become a recurring family joke now, but when Granddad (her father) was admitted a few weeks ago, you can be sure that we kept her away at meal times!

Chapter 6

From the ICU, which was awesome and ultra-modern, I was moved in to Ward B7, which I'd describe as 'Victorian'. I remember saying to my Mum that there was absolutely no way that I was staying there – I am a bit of a snob when it comes to living arrangements, I admit. Little did I know how much 'fun' life on Ward B7 was going to turn out to be.

Ward B7 is a general recovery ward for both the neuro and spinal teams. The main aim here is for people to convalesce. Unfortunately, at the time that I was in, only a few of us were actually convalescing, the rest of the 8 beds were unfortunately full of people who were simply too old to go home and largely abandoned by family, which shocked me terribly.

The daily routine was much the same – you'd be woken up ridiculously early (around 7am) for breakfast and to plan your meals. Nothing would then happen until 09:30 when people would come to gawk at you and sentence you to yet another long day of convalescence and then lunch would arrive some time around 13:00. Once you finished lunch, the place became a bit of a zoo, with people coming to stare at elderly relatives who they didn't want to take home (sadly, I'm not jesting here – on one occasion, an old man's son arrived simply to pay for another week of that stupidly overpriced hospital TV). Tea time would be around 17:00 and then at 18:00, the visitors would all come back until 8pm, at which point we'd all start to settle down and await the pre-bedtime tea and toast offer(!), 5 minutes before lights out.

Once the lights were out, the real fun started. I'm never sure why hospitals do this – they wait for cover of darkness to shift people about and do their checks. After a few days it honestly started to become unbearable – the guy at the end, who hadn't moved all day would suddenly, and loudly, defecate in the bed and the chap next to me would then start shouting via his iPad to go to the toilet or for someone to come move him (unfortunately, he'd lost the power of speech – a couple of us so wanted to get our hands on his iPad so that we could at least change the bloody awful grating voice that it used!). Opposite me was a lovely Indian GP who was in his seventies and had such marvellous life stories to tell. Unfortunately, his bladder wasn't working quite so well, so he'd start shuffling to the bathroom with a giant bag of pee swinging at his side. You could hear him doing the 'slosh-shuffle' for ages.

The staff on ward B7 were nothing short of phenomenal. Although their time was often swallowed up by the challenges of caring for those who were in the wrong place, often to my own detriment, they were clearly very overworked, and unsupported.

I soon got used to taking a back seat owing to these problems – you'd think that recovering from a brain tumour and having a massive hole in your head draining fluid would give you some sort of priority. I think the only time I lost it was when an old, but senior ranking gentleman from the clergy in his 60s was brought in for a regular MRI scan. He kept getting bumped for emergency cases, and he became very vocal and demanding and wanted assistance doing everything – he didn't try to do anything himself. It got a bit frustrating that there I was trying to recover from an operation that probably should have killed me, with me not yet out of the woods, and a guy was demanding so much time simply because he was having a routine MRI scan.

After thirteen days of this same old loop, I decided that I'd had enough and asked to be checked out and allowed to recover at home. It took a lot of pleading and even some tears, but eventually they agreed to it.

Chapter 7

It was so wonderful to be back at home and be cared for by my partner (now husband) Max. Normality was such a blessing and though I was taking 16 pills a day in the morning, it was a far more enjoyable experience than hearing that damn iPad shouting TOILET, TOILET, CRISPS!

Max and I went back to the hospital a few days later, largely to get the results of the biopsy. It kind of ruins the tension when you get there and you're simply handed a form to fill in and you realise you're registering for The Christie. Fortunately, I'm made of stronger stuff, but I felt sorry for anyone who perhaps would have received this news in a similarly inappropriate way/environment.

When we met the Consultant, the diagnosis was confirmed – Medulloblastoma. Apparently, if this was any consolation, that's incredibly rare to have in adults and is normally seen in infants, very often with fatal outcomes.

I was then asked to go for a lumbar puncture to test my spine for any sign of the Cancer spreading around my body. First thing – a lumbar puncture hurts like hell, try to avoid having one if you possibly can, and certainly don't let them have two goes minutes after the initial failed attempt, and the second thing, I couldn't believe it, there I was I the exact same bay where my journey had begun. Same staff, same everything.

The Christie was an experience. Up until this point, my experience had been very singular. Suddenly I rounded a corner, passing through a single waiting room with literally hundreds and hundreds of people – it was like a sea of cancer rushing towards me. This really brought a sense of perspective to my predicament. How the staff there manage to go to work each day is nothing short of a miracle. Even now, two years on, the sight of the Outpatients Waiting Room stuns me.

During my Cancer experience I experienced A LOT of nausea, to the point where I nearly died.

First day back home, and a vision of my hair status in ten-years-time!

Chapter 8

Stemming from the operation, I started to get a lot of crippling nausea, and despite investigating every possible anti-emetic, we found that none of them worked at all. It was serious enough that we had to delay my urgent radiotherapy to instead allow me to see if this nausea would fade.

Instead I ended up desperately dehydrated and admitted in to both A&E (the first time) and The Christie (the second time) and immediately put on life-saving fluids to replace the ones that I was rather violently losing every ten minutes or so. I learnt to live on kids ice-pops as a gentle way of getting fluids in.

The nausea alone was the most defining part of my Cancer experience – it made everything so much worse than it needed to be. I may have had Cancer but dehydration was the thing that nearly killed me.

I'm pleased to say, that it finally went away in December 2015, 18 months after the initial operation. To this day we have no idea what was causing it and why it stopped. My freezer is still full of ice pops.

Chapter 9

Radiotherapy was to be the main way that we were to try finishing Cancer off, having very senior experts divided about whether there was residual disease present or not.

At first, I'll admit that it was exciting – getting the face mask made and seeing all the 'cool' equipment – I'm an absolute geek when it comes to this stuff and have a very enquiring mind.

However, once all the sickness started coming and I had a real sense of restlessness, the daily ritual of radiotherapy was to become Hell on Earth.

At 5 days a week, for 6 weeks, the dosage was high and the frequency intense.

I couldn't walk properly still, and had to be pushed around in the Christie's public wheelchairs. By the end of my stint, I'd given them all names, and more out of a sense of loathing than familiarity. When you're feeling ill the last thing you want to be pushed around in and confined to is a rickety old trolley that has zero steering, and, with four small wheels, no way of being able to be moved by anyone other than someone stood behind you. I remember crawling to the bathroom once to vomit as I had to leave the chair.

I tried to source an image online of these chairs to include here, but alas, so unique are they to The Christie that no matter what search-terms I use on Google Images, nothing remotely as basic comes up!

Despite their rough and ready exterior, I have to praise the porter service at The Christie, once you get to know those chaps you get to have a bit of fun with them and they open up somewhat. They're often a familiar constant in a day of change.

Everyone on Suite 10 who was working in April – June 2014 is an absolute angel. Yes, they're technically radiographers, but they also took nursing their patients very seriously too. The nursing care that I received every morning at 11am, far outweighed what I would receive upstairs in a ward. They absolutely went above and beyond for me and were a massive contribution in getting me where I am today.

Chapter 10

Whilst all of this was going on, I had, in the background, a nightmare with the local patient transport service. They were incredibly unreliable, and coupled with my sickness and gruelling radiotherapy schedule, actually made life worse. I genuinely think that they should be ashamed of themselves and I am glad to hear that they have lost this contract going forward.

My experience was often a very delayed pick-up from home and I was often very lucky if they even bothered to come pick me up after treatment, when I was at my sickest. I'd be left stranded in Department 42 (Transport) for literally hours on end, with absolutely no idea what was going on. This would happen daily – and when you're on an intensive radiotherapy schedule as I was, you really needed that downtime and rest period between sessions – their ineptitude denied me that comfort.

Suffice to say, it took such a toll on my health, that the decision was made to admit me each day so that I could await transport in a much quieter location and receive a hospital lunch and nursing care, which I obviously wasn't getting when dumped in the transport waiting area.

I should add, I do not blame the drivers one bit. In fact, I got to know many of them during my ordeal. I've never seen so many employees so genuinely annoyed with their employer. People who had been there for 15 years were telling me that they felt unable to support the levels of service that the Company had committed to, not through their actions, but through those running the business. Many (if not all I encountered) were considering a change in career.

It's a thankless job, but people like these are amongst the hidden warriors of the NHS.

HOSPITAL FOOD BINGO

Chapter 11

I also got involved with speech therapy and a physiotherapist.

Speech therapy was a lot of fun, as you essentially just sit in your home making crazy sounding noises for an hour or so, whilst some person in sports wear uniform (why?) tries to tell you that you don't look stupid. I wonder if they take bets on the stupid things that they can get their clients to do? Ultimately, their wisdom has paid off dividends, but if you're ever diagnosed with an illness that affects your speech, know that you're in for some comedy!

My physiotherapy was a lot less fun, and after a few weeks, I was sentenced to 10 weeks of 'Balance Class', at 10am every Tuesday, about 5 miles away from home.

Balance Class consists largely of incredibly elderly people and excessively spherical people unable to touch (or see) their toes. It really wasn't the rehab clinic that I needed, that much was clear to me from day one.

Twelve 'stations' would be hastily put together around the room, which you'd visit as many of as you can. They were numbered, and this seemed to cause a lot of confusion for the more elderly of our group, who'd spend ages shuffling along to a station out of sequence and you'd have to break yours to accommodate.

The exercises at the stations were actually good and beneficial, though I would have got a lot more out of them were I given them in a home setting. The main benefit of the sessions was that I got to see my kid sister weekly and have someone to share the stories of horror with when I finished each week.

We also had District Nurses coming around to the apartment once a day to change a syringe driver that was providing me with 24 hour anti-emetics to try and curb the nausea.

For anyone unfamiliar with a syringe driver it's basically a box that you carry around that has a medical syringe in it and a battery powered plunger that was reset each day, and to have delivered 100% of the medication 24 hours later. Daily visits to restock and reset the driver were needed.

I'd love to say that they came to help me, however, soon different nurses started coming and we found out that one of our cats, Pearl, a gorgeous, prize-winnings British Blue, had become a local celebrity amongst our local care team (including the physio and speech therapists). People started picking up my needs simply to come see the cat. It wasn't uncommon to hear one say "look Pamela, it's that cat!" and then spend twenty minutes fawning over it. Indeed, on the occasions the cats were being rowdy and I shut them away, nurses would actually request that I let them out and appear massively disappointed. You haven't lived until someone has emotionally blackmailed you into letting them in to your bedroom just to see your pet.

Chapter 12

I stopped going in for Radiotherapy in June 2014, and things have slowly been getting back to normal. My balance is still a little off, I can't use my left hand for fine motor skills, and I have a lovely dent in my head that I have to warn my hairdresser about when I go to get my hair done.

I can't complain, and never have. I'm one of the lucky ones.

Now in February 2016 I've received a provisional all-clear and life is going great for me. My then partner, Max, was a HUGE support to me during my Cancer experience, and I'm pleased to say that we got married in the summer of 2015. I'm back at work and doing hours that pretty much represent full time, I have a lot more confidence in general and have managed to fundraise some decent amounts to help those who helped me most during this ordeal.

I got lucky and had Critical Illness insurance via my employer. I was awarded £250,000 for my diagnosis. In a way, I feel like I've cheated the system a bit, having come out relatively unscathed (well, I'm not dead, so anything is a bonus really). It has been put to good use, buying my husband and I a house out in the Peak District, with two cats and three chickens. Most importantly, it gives us both some stability in life to hang a full recovery from and security for Max if I were to pass on, that he'll always have a home – I owe him at least that much for the life-saving care that he provided to me and his unwavering love and care.

Despite receiving a diagnosis that was incredibly 'rare', I didn't just survive, I became a new person in my self – **Gari Wellingham, the lad that lived.**

Our Wedding Day – Gari (l) and Max (r)

Original Epilogue

http://garidavies.me.uk/2016/02/14/ive-survived-cancer-havent-i/

I've survived Cancer, haven't I?
FEBRUARY 14, 2016 BY GARI

One of, for me, the trickiest question in the whole 'Cancer' experience.

I guess nobody survives Cancer (whether you've had it before or not) until we die of some other cause, which isn't Cancer.

The question should really be, have my odds of dying from Cancer reached those of a 'normal' person of my age/lifestyle etc.

I've wrestled with the declaration for a number of months – it seems naive to say that I've beat it, but looking at what's been accomplished, it would appear that I have.

The problem is that, though I no longer want to be known as 'that guy who had the rare brain tumour', I worry that as soon as I make this declaration, everyone will just assume that I'm magically up to 100% and if I do, by chance, have the Cancer come back, or develop it in a different place, the second time is going to feel more bitter for my friends and family than it did the first.

Here's my current situation:

- All of my MRI Scans have been clear since July 2014 when I completed radiotherapy. That said, I will be scanned frequently for the next ten years instead of the usual five (which I'm very much in favour of, I'd recommend them for everyone each year on the NHS were they not so expensive!)

- I'm about to trial an increase in working hours which increases my input to 34.5 hours a week – my contract is for 35. It's taken since January 2015 to get to this stage.

- My left hand still lacks the fine co-ordination skills that it had and my co-ordination is still a little wobbly at the best of times – this is just a norm now, left over from the surgery to that part of the brain. They're not anywhere like severe enough to class as a disability, more a minor inconvenience.

So there you have it, my current quandary, I was always told by NHS staff that there is no medical point where you declare that you've survived Cancer, it is just something that "happens" when the time feels right. I 100% agree with this and in my opinion I think nobody ever 'survives' Cancer – they just win the battle and live to fight the next – be it Cancer again or some other disease in the future.

I seemingly get to live to fight another day, *hurrah!*

"There is no glory in illness. There is no meaning to it. There is no honor in 'dying of'.

John Green, The Fault in Our Stars"

Gari Wellingham – Brain Cancer Survivor, Published Writer and now Fashion Supermodel?!

MARCH 25, 2016

Maggie's On The Runway is a fashion and fundraising event which takes place bi-annually at Manchester Airport Visitor Park. The models (including me!) were 50 people who were living with or after a Cancer diagnosis.

We raised over £175,000!

Visit the following website to see the pictures and to hear about Maggie's On The Runway 2018!
http://www.maggiesontherunway.com

LEGO: More than just a 'toy'?

MAY 28, 2017

What I wanted to share was this email that I have just sent to the folks over at LEGO. At 32, and post-cancer, I never thought I'd be so grateful to a 'toy' that I loved as a 5-10 year old!

Hi,

I'm 32 and a few years ago I had Medulloblastoma – basically, a cancerous brain tumour.

Fortunately, I'm very well now and it's very unlikely to return, however it has left me with some dexterity problems in my hands, especially the left, which I have little fine control over at all. I also have a massive amount of fatigue and can't get out to do many of the things that I used to love.

I recently returned to a childhood favourite; LEGO, and have been building up my collection since. I started with a relatively simple dinosaur, did the lighthouse, then the Fire Truck and have just progressed on to LEGO Technic – the big pneumatic digger.

My husband was my rock during this time of having Cancer and my inability to resume the activities that we used to enjoy together (we were both avid hill-walkers, and we live in the Peak District) has been a source of guilt for the last few years.

This bank holiday weekend, we bought the LEGO Technical pneumatic digger and we're about half-way through building it. It's been a great experience for both of us to have a shared hobby to replace the ones that I now struggle to participate in. We've been at it all day today with plans to complete it tomorrow. It's so nice for us to be able to sit down and do something constructive together. (pardon the pun!).

Even better news, the complexity of the build, has forced me to start using my weaker left hand to support building. In effect, it's doing the physio, that I loathe the idea of, for me and not in a way that I resent. It's going to help me in life so much if I can get the dexterity back in my hand!

Thank you for so many lovely LEGO sets, as time and budget permits, I really hope to expand my collection and in doing so, continue to develop in life too.

I know it sounds a bit 'hippy-dippy' – I was surprised to have this revelation too!

I do have one question though – why does this digger not come with a LEGO man to sit in the cab and 'operate' it?

Gari Wellingham

41861022R00019

Printed in Poland
by Amazon Fulfillment
Poland Sp. z o.o., Wrocław

Gari
Wellingham

ISBN 9781549844072

9 781549 844072

THE
BOOTLEGGER

First he fights to save his farm
Then he has to fight to save lives

KEITH LAWSON